HAUNTED BATTLEFIELDS

JANICE DYER

CRABTREE
PUBLISHING COMPANY
WWW.CRABTREEBOOKS.COM

HAUNTED OR HOAX?

Author: Janice Dyer

Editors: Marcia Abramson, Petrice Custance

Photo research: Melissa McClellan

Cover/interior design: T.J. Choleva

Proofreader: Lorna Notsch

**Production coordinator and
 prepress technician:** Tammy McGarr

Print coordinator: Katherine Berti

Consultant: Susan Demeter-St. Clair
 Paranormal Studies & Inquiry

Written and produced for Crabtree Publishing by
BlueAppleWorks Inc.

Library and Archives Canada Cataloguing in Publication

Dyer, Janice, author
  Haunted battlefields / Janice Dyer.

(Haunted or hoax?)
Includes index.
Issued in print and electronic formats.
ISBN 978-0-7787-4628-7 (hardcover).--
ISBN 978-0-7787-4639-3 (softcover).--
ISBN 978-1-4271-2052-6 (HTML)

    1. Haunted places--Juvenile literature. 2. Battlefields--Juvenile
literature. 3. Ghosts--Juvenile literature. I. Title.

BF1461.D94 2018   j133.1'22   C2017-907782-1
                                            C2017-907783-X

Library of Congress Cataloging-in-Publication Data

CIP available at the Library of Congress

Crabtree Publishing Company
www.crabtreebooks.com   1-800-387-7650

Printed in the U.S.A./032018/BG20180202

**Published in Canada
Crabtree Publishing**
616 Welland Ave.
St. Catharines, Ontario
L2M 5V6

**Published in the United States
Crabtree Publishing**
PMB 59051
350 Fifth Avenue, 59th Floor
New York, New York 10118

**Published in the United Kingdom
Crabtree Publishing**
Maritime House
Basin Road North, Hove
BN41 1WR

**Published in Australia
Crabtree Publishing**
3 Charles Street
Coburg North
VIC, 3058

CONTENTS

FIELDS OF VIOLENT DEATHS

Since ancient times, people have told stories of ghosts and ghostly sightings. Many believe that ghosts are the souls or spirits of people who can't find rest after they have died. Ghosts are said to haunt many different locations, such buildings, ships, and graveyards.

To make sure that a dead person's spirit would not return to haunt the living, many cultures started using funerals as a way to provide a soul with a safe passage to the afterlife.

Deadly Past

Some locations are more likely to be haunted than others. Battlefields are one example of such places. Why do you suppose that is? Perhaps it is because of the violent deaths and bloodshed that occurred on this land in the past. Big battles were mostly fought on open fields. However, haunted battlefields are usually reported to be ones with difficult **terrain**, where the battles were especially bloody.

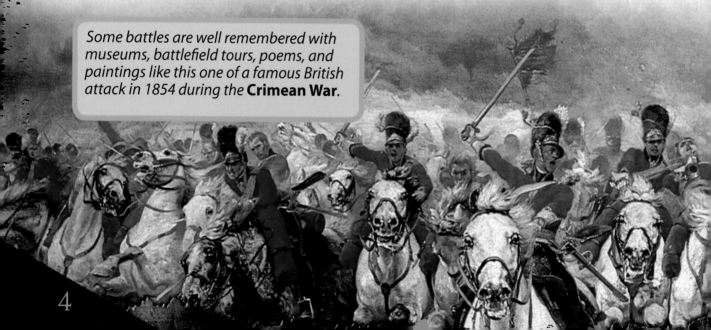

Some battles are well remembered with museums, battlefield tours, poems, and paintings like this one of a famous British attack in 1854 during the **Crimean War**.

Haunted or Hoax?

Some ghost sightings on battlefields may be caused by unknown **paranormal** forces. A paranormal event is one that cannot be explained by normal experiences or by science. Things like ghosts, unidentified flying objects (UFOs), **psychic** abilities, and **extraterrestrial** life are all referred to as paranormal.

But do ghosts really exist? Most of the **evidence** is only **anecdotal**, which means it is based on people's stories, rather than on scientific proof. Even so, stories of ghosts have continued to be shared through the ages. Most cultures make some reference to ghosts in their **legends** and stories passed down from earlier times.

In reality, many of the ghost sightings reported on battlefields are **hoaxes**, made up to trick people or attract attention. Tourists may be more likely to visit a particular battlefield if there are reports that it is haunted. So people in the area may make up stories or exaggerate events to encourage people to visit.

The best paranormal investigators look for simple explanations, as well as ghostly ones. They keep an open mind as they spend long hours studying evidence.

THE CIVIL WAR'S BLOODIEST BATTLES

The Battle of Gettysburg was the bloodiest battle of the U.S. **Civil War**. From July 1 to 3, 1863, more than 94,000 **Union** troops fought against 72,000 **Confederate** soldiers on this battlefield in southern Pennsylvania. On July 3, the Confederates launched an attack known as Pickett's Charge, but it was a devastating failure.

Cannons and heavy gunfire killed many troops. Soldiers used their rifles, **bayonets**, rocks, and even their bare hands in hand-to-hand combat. More than 50,000 Americans were killed, wounded, or went missing during the three days of fighting.

DID YOU KNOW?

Mary Virginia Wade ("Jennie" or "Ginnie") was the only resident of Gettysburg killed during the battle. A stray bullet hit her house during the battle and killed her while she was baking bread to feed the soldiers. It is said that her ghost comforts people who are scared or upset.

Pickett's Charge, named after General George Pickett, inspired this 1887 painting as well as legends and ghost stories.

After the Battle

When the battle ended, the streets of Gettysburg and its surrounding fields were covered with the bodies of the dead. The town of Gettysburg had only 2,400 residents at the time. They treated thousands of wounded soldiers. They turned their homes and other buildings into hospitals. The residents were overwhelmed with the number of injured and dying soldiers.

The new art of photography allowed the whole world to see close-up images from Civil War battlefields. Those who lost loved ones sometimes looked for their ghosts in the photos.

On November 19, 1863, President Abraham Lincoln spoke to the nation at the dedication of a Union cemetery near Gettysburg. His famous speech is known as the Gettysburg Address. Lincoln first honored the soldiers who died there. He said they were fighting to keep the country together and to uphold the ideals of liberty and equality. Then he asked Americans to keep striving for those ideals, just as the brave soldiers at Gettysburg had.

*Abraham Lincoln also may be a ghost of the Civil War. He was **assassinated** in 1865. Since then, people have reported feeling or seeing his ghost at the White House.*

Paranormal Events

Today, when people hear the name "Gettysburg," many of them think of haunted buildings and ghostly sightings on the battlefield. Even if they don't believe in ghosts, people often talk about experiencing spooky feelings while touring Gettysburg. Visitors over the years have reported ghostly stories and encounters with ghosts of soldiers who were part of the bloody battle.

Many of the buildings used as hospitals after the battle are also said to be haunted. Others claim to have seen ghost soldiers and ghost battles in the fields around Gettysburg.

The Daniel Lady Farm served as a Confederate hospital at Gettysburg. Many believe that more than 10,000 dead soldiers haunt the grounds.

Ghosts of Cashtown Inn

The owners of the Cashtown Inn claim to have photographic evidence of spirits in the building. Guests also report hearing knocking on doors, seeing lights turn on and off, and hearing doors lock and unlock themselves.

Hauntings in Pennsylvania Hall

The Confederates used Pennsylvania Hall, Gettysburg College's oldest building, as a field hospital and look-out post during the battle. Soldiers watched the progress of the battle from the **cupola**, a small dome structure, on the top of the building. On certain nights, students living in the hall today report seeing figures of soldiers pacing back and forth in the cupola.

The Devil's Den is called the most haunted part of the Gettysburg battlefield. Visitors often report seeing and hearing the ghosts of soldiers killed in action. Some even say their cameras and video equipment stopped working properly in part of this area. Even during the battle, in letters to their families, soldiers called the area a "desolate and ghostly place."

ANTIETAM, MARYLAND, USA

Antietam was the bloodiest one-day battle in the American Civil War. The battle lasted only four hours on September 17, 1862, and took place on a road between two farms in Maryland. More than 23,000 men were killed, wounded, or missing in action. Today, the road is called Bloody Lane. Visitors to the area often report the sound of gunfire and smell of gunpowder. Many claim to have both seen and heard spirits in the area. Most areas surrounding the Battle of Antietam have had reports of hauntings, including a nearby bridge and two houses that stand on the battlefield.

Today, eight different companies offer ghost tours in and around Gettysburg.

LOOK AT THE EVIDENCE

Experts say there is no real evidence that the Gettysburg battlefield is haunted. A "spooky feeling" isn't actual proof of paranormal activity. What could have caused people to report the hauntings and sightings? Experts say that the ghost stories surrounding the Battle of Gettysburg became more popular in the 1990s, just when people started making more money on ghost books and tours. What do you think?

GHOSTS OF THE PLAINS

The Seven Years' War (1756–1763) took place between Britain and France in their **colonies** around the world. In what is now called North America, Britain fought to win control of the French colonies.

The head of the British forces, James Wolfe, decided to attack the fortress city of Québec, in present-day Canada, in 1759. The Marquis de Montcalm's troops were guarding the city for France. The Plains of Abraham was the site of the historic showdown between the French and British armies that occurred on September 13, 1759.

The British forces blocked supply routes and communication before the battle to weaken the French troops.

Bloody Battle

The night before the battle, Wolfe's army landed upstream of Québec City. They climbed a tall, steep cliff and overtook the small French army guarding the area. By daybreak, 4,500 British soldiers were on the Plains of Abraham. Montcalm's army was about the same size.

The battle lasted less than an hour. The British soldiers held their fire until the French forces were within 90 feet (27 meters). The British fired their guns quickly, moved forward, then fired again. The French forces suffered heavy losses. Britain won the battle, and also the war.

More than 1,000 men died on that September day. Hundreds more were wounded. General Wolfe died within the first few minutes of the battle. General Montcalm was wounded, and he died the next day.

The French did not prepare for the British climbing the cliff because they thought it couldn't be done.

According to legend, General Wolfe died after hearing that his forces were winning. His last words were, "Now, I will die in peace."

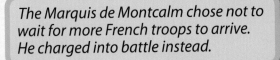

The Marquis de Montcalm chose not to wait for more French troops to arrive. He charged into battle instead.

Paranormal Events

It's not surprising that with so much violent loss of life in such a short time, many consider the Plains of Abraham to be the most haunted place in Québec. September, the month the battle occurred, is considered to be the spookiest time to visit the area because of an increase in paranormal activity.

There have been numerous ghost sightings across the old battlefield and near the **barracks**, especially around the anniversary of the battle. Visitors have reported seeing the ghosts of troops and smelling gunpowder in the nearby tunnels. Others say they have heard cannon fire and felt as though something (or someone!) had brushed up against them. Some even report hearing sounds of dying men and horses.

It is said that the grass on the Plains of Abraham is green and lush today because of how much blood was spilled there in 1759.

La Corriveau

Another ghost that people claim is haunting the Plains of Abraham is that of Marie-Josephte Corriveau. She is called "La Corriveau" in Québécois **folklore**. Marie was executed in 1763 for murdering her husband with a hatchet. She was hanged near the Plains of Abraham, and her body was displayed for a month along a busy road in Québec City. The body was chained and hung in an iron cage to show what happens to murderers. People were frightened by the sight. A legend soon spread about Marie's angry spirit walking along the road. People said she would open her blood-red eyes and try to grab travelers. Even now, some people report seeing a skeletal ghost of Marie.

Marie-Josephte Corriveau is such a famous ghost that she was chosen to appear on a 2015 postage stamp in the Haunted Canada series.

During the War of 1812, American forces took control of southern Ontario. They camped on the Gage family farm, and tied up the Gage family in the basement. Billy Green, a local 19-year-old, saw what was happening and warned the British. The British army made a surprise attack on the American soldiers and won the battle. People say the Gage farm in Stoney Creek is haunted not only by dead soldiers, but also by Mary Jones Gage, the farm's owner. Her home is now a museum. Employees and visitors report that pieces of furniture and other antiques often vanish. Then they reappear later in another part of the house. In addition to Mary haunting the actual home, visitors report seeing ghostly, misty soldiers walking across the field. Some also hear the sound of cannons firing.

LOOK AT THE EVIDENCE

Evidence of ghost sightings at the Plains of Abraham is based on the statements of witnesses. The Plains of Abraham are often foggy. Is it possible that people are mistaking fog for ghosts? This battlefield was preserved as a national park in 1908. Millions of tourists visit it every year. Are you convinced by these stories, or could they be made up to attract tourists to the area?

CHILLING HAUNTINGS
OF COLD HARBOR

The Battle of Cold Harbor was one of the Civil War's bloodiest battles. Thousands of Union soldiers were killed in attacks against the **fortified** positions of the Confederate army. The battle took place from May 31 to June 12, 1864.

Killing Grounds

Before the battle, Confederate general Robert E. Lee's army had built an elaborate series of **trenches** at Old Cold Harbor near Richmond, Virginia. When Lieutenant General Ulysses S. Grant attempted to take the area, his troops were slaughtered. More than 7,000 Union soldiers were killed or injured in the first hour of battle alone. About 16,000 men were killed, wounded, reported missing, or captured over the course of the entire battle. The two armies fought each other for nine days before the Union army left the area.

DID YOU KNOW?

The Battle of Cold Harbor was a miserable experience. The area was heavily wooded and the ground was uneven, making it difficult for fighting. There was limited food and water for the soldiers and also a shortage of medical help.

The Union general, Ulysses S. Grant, deeply regretted the attack.

General Robert E. Lee commanded the Confederate States army.

14

Paranormal Events

Locals have reported hearing artillery fire and shouts of men and smelling gunpowder. Many have also come upon a thick fog that quickly surrounds the area and then just as quickly disappears. Some people believe that so many ghosts have been reported at Cold Harbor because there was no time to dig proper graves for the dead. The result? Unsettled spirits that haunt the area.

The Civil War troops took over the Garthright House not once but twice. It also was used as a hospital in the Battle of Gaines' Mill in 1862.

Child Ghost of Cold Harbor

The Garthright House was located near the battlefield. Union doctors used it as a hospital during the battle. The family was forced to stay in the basement and heard soldiers crying out in pain. At the end of the battle, 97 soldiers were buried under the front lawn of the house. Visitors today report that the home is haunted by a little girl, called the Child Ghost of Cold Harbor. They say the ghost of the little girl wears a white dress and bonnet. She wanders through the meadows and graveyards near the battlefield or peers out from a window of the Garthright House. Some believe she is one of the family members who lived in the house during the battle.

LOOK AT THE EVIDENCE

Evidence of ghost sightings at Cold Harbor is based on the statements of witnesses. Some investigators have also used cameras, night vision equipment, and other technology to try to record paranormal events. They found some light irregularities in several of the photographs. Today, part of the battlefield is preserved as a park, including the 7 miles (11 km) of trench system. Are you convinced by these stories, or could they be made up to attract tourists to the area?

THE LITTLE BIGHORN MASSACRE

The Battle of the Little Bighorn took place on June 25 and 26, 1876, in Montana. Lieutenant Colonel George Armstrong Custer led more than 200 U.S. soldiers against about 3,000 Native American warriors. Gold had been found in the area, so the U.S. government wanted to claim the land around Little Bighorn and force the Native Americans onto **reservations**. Custer and all his men died during the battle.

Despite the victory of the Native Americans during the Battle of the Little Bighorn, within five years most Native Americans were living on reservations.

DID YOU KNOW?

Custer became a hero during the Civil War. People spoke of "Custer's luck" because his daring plans worked and he never seemed to get hurt. At Gettysburg, he bravely led his cavalry to help stop Pickett's Charge.

Custer was also reckless. He knew he was far outnumbered but fought anyway at the Battle of the Little Bighorn, resulting in the death of himself and every one of his men. The battle became known as Custer's Last Stand.

Ghostly Warriors

The Custer National Cemetery, where 5,000 veterans and their families are buried, is located beside the battlefield. Visitors and employees at the national park believe the dead are restless. They report seeing soldiers and Native warriors fighting to the death, and Native warriors dressed for war. They also say they have seen shadowy figures of U.S. soldiers on the battlefield and in the buildings located on the grounds. Others report sudden drops in temperature and murmuring voices.

The graveyard at Little Bighorn became an official national cemetery in 1886. Soldiers and veterans from later wars are also buried there.

At first, this simple memorial marked the area where Custer and his men died. Later, a tall stone **obelisk** was built. In 1877, Custer's body was moved to West Point, the U.S. military academy, but some say his ghost haunts the museum at Little Bighorn to this day.

LOOK OUT! GHOST TERRITORY!

What happens when multiple disasters and tragedies happen in one specific location? According to some, the result is multiple reports of hauntings and paranormal activities! The **peninsula** of Point Lookout, Maryland, is one of these locations—shipwrecks, fire, famine, disease, and war have all occurred there over the years.

Camp Misery

Point Lookout was used as a camp for prisoners of war and a hospital for the wounded from the Battle of Gettysburg. It was built for 10,000 men but often held twice as many. The prisoners lacked clothing, shelter, food, clean water, and firewood. Many died of diseases that spread through the camp. They were buried in mass graves, along with those who died of wounds from battle.

Point Lookout was also part of the **Underground Railroad.** Escaped slaves from Virginia used it as a stop on their way north.

Haunted Lighthouse

Many ship passengers and sailors have died during storms and hurricanes near Point Lookout. A lighthouse was built in 1830 to try to prevent these tragedies. The first four lighthouse keepers died while on duty, and ship disasters continued to occur.

Many paranormal investigators have explored the Point Lookout Lighthouse.

The Point Lookout Lighthouse has been called the most haunted lighthouse in America. Visitors report seeing the ghost of a woman wearing a white blouse and long blue skirt. They believe she may be one of the lighthouse keepers who died there.

Witnesses say they have heard moans, slamming doors, and the sound of objects crashing to the ground in the lighthouse. Lighthouse workers also have said they heard heavy footsteps in the hallway and smelled strange smells.

Many of the ghostly sightings around the lighthouse and nearby cemetery are of Confederate and Union soldiers. Witnesses report seeing a man in Civil War clothing moving across the road. They describe him as smelling of mildew and gunpowder. Others have heard sounds of shipwrecked sailors and captive soldiers.

FORT WILLIAM HENRY, NEW YORK, USA

Experts call Fort William Henry one of the most haunted military sites in America. They believe the paranormal activity reported in the area is due to the horrible massacre that happened there in the 1700s during the French and Indian War. Native Americans and French soldiers attacked the fort and killed British and Colonial troops, as well as women and children. Many of the guides who work at the fort today describe feeling that someone is trying to get their attention. They also report hearing footsteps and brushing up against something. The fort has even been featured on the television show *Ghost Hunters*.

LOOK AT THE EVIDENCE

Paranormal researchers have used technology to record the sounds and noises around the Point Lookout Lighthouse. The recordings have picked up 24 different sounds, including shutters slamming in the wind. The wind was not blowing at the time and the shutters had been removed years before. The area is marshy and wet, so the ghost sightings could be explained by people seeing shapes in thick fog. But what about the sounds? What do you think could explain them?

In 1746, two families laid claim to the throne of England. Charles Stuart's family had been replaced on the throne by the Hanovers. Charles wanted his family's throne back. He called on his loyal supporters, called Jacobites, to form an army. They vowed to fight for their "Bonnie Prince Charlie" against the Hanover king, George II.

Battle for a Throne

Charles and his army met the king's army at a place called Culloden in Scotland. The armies clashed on a large, soggy field called a moor. But the odds were against Charles. His army was outnumbered by the king's forces. Tired after marching for many days, his army was quickly wiped out in a fierce, bloody battle. More than 1,500 soldiers were slaughtered in less than an hour.

Any Jacobite who escaped was hunted down and killed by the king's soldiers.

The battlefield at Culloden was filled with the dead.

Battle of Ghosts

EERIE GRAVEYARD

The soldiers who died at Culloden were buried on the moor with gravestones that identified their clan, or family. There is a popular belief that birds will not sing and heather (at right) will not grow near the graves.

But the battle isn't over. Locals in Culloden have claimed to see the battle being fought again by ghostly soldiers. They say they have heard the ringing of swords and moaning of the wounded. The sightings occurred mostly in the first years following the battle on its anniversary. But even 200 years later, a woman saw a **tartan** cloth like those worn by Scottish Highlanders in Charles' army on one of the graves. When she picked it up, she saw the ghost of a wounded soldier underneath. Others have seen the ghost of a tall man in a kilt who whispers the word "defeated."

LOOK AT THE EVIDENCE

Evidence of the ghost sightings at Culloden is based on the statements of witnesses. The area is marshy and wet. It is often foggy. Could shapes seen through thick fog be mistaken for ghosts? The battlefield is now a historic site. Are you convinced by these stories, or could they be made up to attract tourists?

CLAN MACKINTOSH

21

SNOWFALL GHOSTS

During the winter of 1460–61, two groups were fighting for control of England. The Lancastrians were loyal to the king, Henry VI. The Yorkists supported the king's cousin, the Duke of York, and his son Edward. The two sides met in a battle for the crown on March 29, 1461, in a field near the town of Towton.

Battle of Towton

The Battle of Towton took place in the middle of snow, sleet, wind, and bitter cold. When the battle began, the Yorkists were heavily outnumbered. The two sides began their battle using bows and arrows and the earliest form of handguns. Then the king's supporters advanced and began bloody hand-to-hand combat with the Yorkists. The two sides were evenly matched, until extra soldiers arrived who supported Edward.

Over the next 10 hours, Edward's army overcame its enemy, killing soldiers even as they tried to escape in defeat. Estimates are that 28,000 men were killed in what is known as Bloody Meadow. They were buried in mass graves.

An ancient cross was turned into a memorial at Towton in 1931. In this area, locals say they can sometimes hear the groaning of dying soldiers.

LOOK AT THE EVIDENCE

Evidence of the ghost sightings at Towton is based on statements of witnesses. Can you think of anything that could explain the sightings? Are you convinced by the stories, or do you think they are made up?

Historians say the Battle of Towton, on March 29, 1461, was the most brutal battle ever fought in England.

The Legend of Towton

The battle took place during a heavy snowstorm. The legend of Towton states that once every seven years a similar storm occurs. During the heavy snowfall, two ghostly armies can be seen battling for three hours and 12 minutes. Then the armies aren't seen for another seven years. Other locals report seeing ghost soldiers in the woods around the battlefield and near the creek.

One of the pubs in the area also regularly reports paranormal events. Locals refer to the ghost as "Nancy" and say she is responsible for "odd" events that have happened. For example, they blame her for tipping over dishes and moving pots and bottles around the pub.

The owners say Nancy makes mischief but is not scary—and she is just one of the old pub's ghosts!

GHOSTLY MONKS

In 1066, Harold, king of England, and William, Duke of Normandy, were fighting for control of the crown. Each had an army of between 5,000 and 7,000 men. The Battle of Hastings took place on October 14 in East Sussex, England. It lasted all day.

Hundred of people gather every October to act out the Battle of Hastings in full costume. Thousands more come from all over the world to watch.

Norman Rule

William's army, the Normans, pretended to flee in panic but then turned on their enemy. This strategy led to the Normans eventually overtaking the English. Harold was killed at the end of the battle. William became known as William the Conqueror and became king of England until his death.

Some experts say that thousands of soldiers from both sides died during the epic battle, though the exact number is unknown. The dead were buried in mass graves.

MARSTON MOOR, ENGLAND

The Battle of Marston Moor took place on July 2, 1644, during a thunderstorm. It was a vicious battle between Royalists, who supported the king, and Parliamentarians, who wanted no king at all. More than 4,000 soldiers died, mostly Royalists. They were buried in mass graves without a ceremony or memorial. Witnesses claim to have seen the ghosts of blood-stained soldiers on horseback, along with a headless soldier looking for the battle. Others report seeing the ghost of Oliver Cromwell, who led the winning side in the battle. They say he staggers through the moor, trying to escape the spirits of the men killed there by his army.

Oliver Cromwell eventually was named Lord Protector and ruled until he died in 1658.

Building the Abbey

King William decided to build an **abbey**, now called Battle Abbey, on the site of the battle as a memorial to the dead. He also wanted to **make amends** for the bloodshed that had occurred during the battle. He made sure that the altar of the church was placed to mark where Harold had died during the Battle of Hastings.

The king decided that 60 **monks** would live in the abbey. The monks lived in peace for years, praying, reading, and working the land. Years later, Henry VIII took over the abbey and gave it to his friend, Sir Anthony Browne, who took its treasures and then destroyed the church. It is said that he used the stones from the abbey to build a massive house for himself.

A legend says that the grass at Battle Abbey turns blood-red in rain. But this may be caused by iron in the soil.

Visitors often report seeing monks near the abbey. Workers at the abbey say there are no longer any monks there. What do you think the visitors are seeing?

Paranormal Events

Legend tells of the ghost of King Harold staggering around the abbey grounds with an arrow in his eye. On the anniversary of the battle, witnesses report seeing a knight riding across the battlefield and hearing the sounds of battle taking place nearby. Some people also claim to have seen the ghost of a woman wearing a red dress roaming the abbey grounds.

Dozens of others report stories of ghostly monks wandering through the buildings. Specifically, the Black Monk is said to haunt the archways and hallways at Battle Abbey. Ghostly monks who are chanting are another common sighting in the abbey.

MONK'S CURSE

Henry VIII thought he was doing a big favor for his pal Sir Anthony Browne. But his gift of Battle Abbey brought down a curse on Browne's family.

When Sir Anthony took over Battle Abbey, he didn't care that it had been a holy place. He caused so much destruction that he was cursed by the last monk to leave the site.

Sir Anthony was having a feast at the mansion he built from the abbey's stones. According to legend, the sad monk loudly said, "By fire and water, thy line shall come to an end and it shall perish out of this land."

For a long while, the curse did not seem to work. The Browne family sold Battle Abbey in 1721. Perhaps they thought they would escape the curse. In 1793, though, their home at Cowdray Hall burned down. Many precious items looted from the abbey were destroyed. Soon after, the last male directly descended from Sir Anthony drowned in Germany. As foretold by the sad monk, Sir Anthony's family line had died out.

LOOK AT THE EVIDENCE

Photographs have been taken of paranormal events occurring in and around Battle Abbey. One shows the shadowy outline of a monk wearing a hood. Other evidence of ghost sightings is based on the statements of witnesses. Do you think the abbey is haunted? What do you think could explain these ghost sightings?

WHAT DO YOU THINK?

Are ghosts real or are they a hoax?

Many cultures around the world believe in ghosts, along with millions of people. Some find it comforting to think that the spirits of their loved ones are looking out for them during their times of need.

Popular television shows like *Ghost Hunters* encourage people to believe in ghosts by saying that any unexplained light or noise could be evidence of ghosts. They may use high-tech scientific equipment, but that doesn't mean that paranormal investigators are actually detecting ghosts.

DID YOU KNOW?

Ghost stories have been told worldwide since ancient times. In these tales, spirits are dead people or animals that reappear. Such ghosts are mostly harmless. Other kinds of ghosts, called poltergeists, make noise and move things. They are even known to have the ability to attack people at times. All these tales are folklore and have not been proven true—yet.

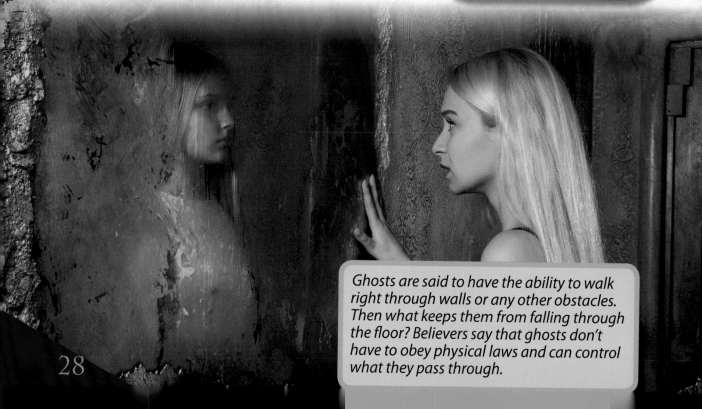

Ghosts are said to have the ability to walk right through walls or any other obstacles. Then what keeps them from falling through the floor? Believers say that ghosts don't have to obey physical laws and can control what they pass through.

Ghostly Lure

Over time, people have even started using "ghosts" as an explanation for something that is unexplainable. Did the door close on its own? Are your keys missing? Is there a cold area in a room? Blame it on a ghost.

Some occurrences may be caused by unknown, paranormal forces that scientists have not yet been able to prove. But some are hoaxes created and continued by people to attract attention. The increase in tourism to "haunted" buildings and battlefields is one reason for doing this.

GHOSTLY THOUGHTS

Some people think that ghosts and ghost hunters are all hoaxes. Ghost hunters usually say they base their work on science. They use a lot of high-tech equipment, including motion detectors, magnetic sensors, thermometers, and video and audio recorders. But what are they capturing with their fancy devices? No one has ever been able to prove the existence of a ghost.

Some claim the right equipment to detect ghosts has not been invented yet. Others say the spirit world is not meant to be detected, but it's still there. In this view, spirits are like ideas. They cannot be heard or seen but certainly exist.

These different beliefs raise some ghostly questions. If ghosts truly have a physical presence, shouldn't there be a scientific way to detect it? If they exist but can never be detected, why bother hunting them?

People may never know the answers to these questions. What do you think?

FAMOUS HOAXES

WILLIAM H. MUMLER– SPIRIT PHOTOGRAPHER

Spirit photography became popular in the 1800s. William Mumler was a famous spirit photographer in New York and Boston. He took photos of people whose relatives had died during the Civil War. He made it look like the spirits of their dead relatives were also in the photos. People were comforted thinking that their dead relatives lived on. One of his most famous photos was of Mary Todd Lincoln with the ghostly image of President Lincoln in the background.

In reality, Mumler used a double exposure technique to create the ghostly image in his photos. When people discovered some of the so-called ghosts were alive, Mumler was tried in court for **fraud**. He was found not guilty due to a lack of evidence. But he never recovered from the debt he went into defending himself.

Today, everyone knows that Mumler's photos are fakes. Yet, at the time, people were fascinated by the photographs. They thought the photos were evidence of the existence of ghosts.

One of the fake Mumler's photographs showing Mary Todd Lincoln with the "ghost" of her husband, Abraham Lincoln.

BOOKS

Haunted Battlefields by Dan Asfar. Ghost House Books, 2004.

Haunted Battlefields and Cemeteries by Alex Summers. Rourke Pub Group, 2016.

Haunted! Gettysburg by Michael Rajczak. Gareth Stevens, 2013.

Little Bighorn: History and Legend by Earle Rice Jr. Purple Toad Publishing, 2015.

WEBSITES

Battle of Hastings
www.bbc.co.uk/history/british/normans/

Civil War Batttles
www.mrnussbaum.com/civil-war/battles/

Wars and Battles through History
www.thoughtco.com/battles-and-wars-throughout-history-4133283

Haunted Rooms: Most Haunted Places in America
www.hauntedrooms.com/haunted-places